U.S. Territories and Possessions

Jada Bradley

Mason Crest
450 Parkway Drive, Suite D
Broomall, PA 19008
www.masoncrest.com

©2016 by Mason Crest, an imprint of National Highlights, Inc.

Printed and bound in the United States of America.

CPSIA Compliance Information: Batch #LES2015.
For further information, contact Mason Crest at 1-866-MCP-Book.

First printing
1 3 5 7 9 8 6 4 2

Library of Congress Cataloging-in-Publication Data

Bradley, Jada.
 U.S. territories and possessions / Jada Bradley.
    pages cm. — (Let's explore the states)
 Includes bibliographical references and index.
 ISBN 978-1-4222-3335-1 (hc)
 ISBN 978-1-4222-8620-3 (ebook)
 1. United States—Territories and possessions—Juvenile literature.
 2. United States—Insular possessions—Juvenile literature. I. Title.
 F965.B73 2016
 909'.091973—dc23

                              2015008419

Let's Explore the States series ISBN: 978-1-4222-3319-1

About the Author: Jada Bradley is a writer and reader who loves to learn. Originally from Buffalo, New York, she now lives in the Washington, D.C., area.

Picture Credits: Library of Congress: 13, 30; National Archives: 40, 50; National Park Service: 60, 61; used under license from Shutterstock, Inc.: 1, 5, 6, 9, 11, 12, 16, 19 (bottom), 20, 21, 24, 27, 28, 31, 32, 33, 36, 39, 46, 49, 51, 52, 54, 57 (top); Aspen Photo / Shutterstock.com: 17 (bottom); S. Bukley / Shutterstock.com: 17 (top); Everett Collection / Shutterstock.com: 58; A. Katz / Shutterstock.com: 19 (top); Venturelli Luca / Shutterstock.com: 14; Chad Zuber / Shutterstock.com: 15; U.S. Air Force photo: 41, 44; U.S. Coast Guard photo: 57 (bottom); U.S. Department of Defense: 59.

Table of Contents

Puerto Rico 7

U.S. Virgin Islands 25

Guam 37

Northern Mariana Islands...47

American Samoa 55

Index 63

Series Glossary 64

KEY ICONS TO LOOK FOR:

Words to Understand: These words with their easy-to-understand definitions will increase the reader's understanding of the text, while building vocabulary skills.

Sidebars: This boxed material within the main text allows readers to build knowledge, gain insights, explore possibilities, and broaden their perspectives by weaving together additional information to provide realistic and holistic perspectives.

Research Projects: Readers are pointed toward areas of further inquiry connected to each chapter. Suggestions are provided for projects that encourage deeper research and analysis.

Text-Dependent Questions: These questions send the reader back to the text for more careful attention to the evidence presented there.

Series Glossary of Key Terms: This back-of-the book glossary contains terminology used throughout this series. Words found here increase the reader's ability to read and comprehend higher-level books and articles in this field.

LET'S EXPLORE THE STATES

Atlantic: North Carolina, Virginia, West Virginia

Central Mississippi River Basin: Arkansas, Iowa, Missouri

East South-Central States: Kentucky, Tennessee

Eastern Great Lakes: Indiana, Michigan, Ohio

Gulf States: Alabama, Louisiana, Mississippi

Lower Atlantic: Florida, Georgia, South Carolina

Lower Plains: Kansas, Nebraska

Mid-Atlantic: Delaware, District of Columbia, Maryland

Non-Continental: Alaska, Hawaii

Northern New England: Maine, New Hampshire, Vermont

Northeast: New Jersey, New York, Pennsylvania

Northwest: Idaho, Oregon, Washington

Rocky Mountain: Colorado, Utah, Wyoming

Southern New England: Connecticut, Massachusetts, Rhode Island

Southwest: New Mexico, Oklahoma, Texas

U.S. Territories and Possessions

Upper Plains: Montana, North Dakota, South Dakota

The West: Arizona, California, Nevada

Western Great Lakes: Illinois, Minnesota, Wisconsin

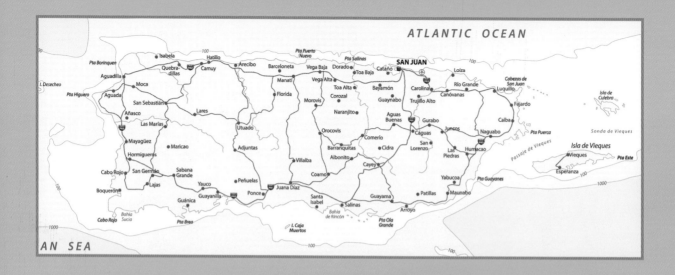

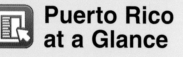

Puerto Rico at a Glance

Area: 5,324 sq miles (13,790 sq km)[1]
  Land: 3,425 sq miles (8,870 sq km)
  Water: 1,900 sq miles (4,921 sq km)
Highest elevation: Cerro de Punto,
  4,390 feet (1,338 m)
Lowest elevation: sea level

Capital: San Juan

Population: 3,548,397[2]

Official bird: stripe-headed tanager
Official flower: Puerto Rican hibiscus

Unofficial mascot: coquí

[1] *U.S. Census Bureau*
[2] *U.S. Census Bureau, 2014 estimate*

Puerto Rico

I t now has the nickname *isla de encanto* (island of enchantment) and the official name of Puerto Rico but this island that is located midway between North and South America has had several names over the centuries, including Borinquen and San Juan Bautista (St. John the Baptist).

Geography

Puerto Rico is the visible part of an underwater mountain that was once a volcano. Puerto Rico has many mountains and hills that contribute toward its varied landscape which ranges from tropical rain forest in the interior to dry land on the southern coast. The island also has more than a dozen artificial lakes that were created during the 20th century.

The dry season in Puerto Rico is from December to April while the wet season extends from May to November. At times, parts of the island are flooded during the wet season. Puerto Rico is also vulnerable to hurricanes.

When European explorers arrived, the island was heavily forested but much of the forest has been cut down over the centuries. While Spain controlled the island, the Spanish government started an initiative to plant more trees. The U.S., which now controls the island, has also made efforts to protect Puerto Rico's forests.

The destruction of forests has not meant the destruction of animal life, however. Puerto Rico is home to more than 200 species of birds. Many species of insects also thrive in its climate. Many kinds of fish and sea creatures can be found in the waters that surround the island.

Perhaps Puerto Rico's most famous animal is the coquí, a tiny tree frog named for the sound it makes ("ko-kee").

 # Words to Understand in This Chapter

Arawak—name for a group of Native American tribes that migrated from South America to various Caribbean islands before the arrival of Europeans.

Carib—a Native American tribe that lived on the coast of South America and attacked the Arawak on Caribbean islands. The word *Caribbean* is derived from their name.

component—one part of something.

creole—a term used during the Spanish colonial era to describe a person of Spanish descent who was born in the colony, not in Spain.

indigenous—something that is produced or occurs naturally in a certain area. This word can be used to describe people who are native to a certain region.

infrastructure—basic resources or systems a country needs to function.

mestizo—a Spanish word for a person of mixed heritage, usually Spanish and native.

Nuyorican—combines New York and Puerto Rican, used to describe people or things that blend New York City culture with Puerto Rican culture.

offshoot—a branch or group that descends from a larger family or social group.

Taino—a Native American tribe of the Caribbean region that spoke the Arawak language.

tax break—a savings on taxes owed provided by a government.

A cloud-covered mountain near the city of San Juan.

Small boats are anchored at Isla Culebra, a small island about 17 miles (27 km) off the coast of Puerto Rico. In addition to the main island, the Commonwealth of Puerto Rico includes a number of small islands, including Culebra, Vieques, and Mona.

History

Archaeologists have found evidence that Puerto Rico was home to several **indigenous** groups. While the **Taino**, a Native American tribe that came in contact with European explorers, are the most well-known, there were several other groups to inhabit the island before the Taino.

Evidence of a first century culture referred to as the Archaics has been found near San Juan and it is not certain whether the Archaics migrated from another Caribbean island or from South America.

More is known about the Igneri or Saladoid people who were more sophisticated than the Archaics and very

skilled at making pottery. This group that came from South America and settled near the coasts may have been conquered by other indigenous groups that also migrated from South America. It is also possible that they may have moved further inland and over time become the Ostionoid people.

The Ostionoids were more advanced than the Igneri. Scholars think they made less pottery and more stone objects. It is also believed that the Taino incorporated some of the Ostionoids' religion and social structure into their culture.

The Taino people of Puerto Rico are an **offshoot** of a larger group called the **Arawak**. The Tainos of Puerto Rico had a language and culture in common with the Tainos that also settled other Caribbean islands, including nearby island of Hispaniola (the land mass that contains Haiti and the Dominican Republic). Taino society had two classes. In the ruling class, power was usually passed through the mother's side of a family.

By the time Christopher Columbus arrived in 1493, the Tainos had

 Did You Know?

The Taino people played a ball game that has some elements in common with modern soccer. Players could use feet and other body parts to move the ball, but they were not allowed to use their hands.

The Spanish built this fort, known as Morro Castle, to defend Puerto Rico in the 16th century.

worked to develop weapons and it is believed that they did so in order to fight off the **Carib** Indians who had begun to attack the island. The Taino did not survive European conquest but some of their language lives on in words like *canoa* (canoe), *barbacoa* (barbecue), *hamaca* (hammock), and *huracan* (hurricane). The Taino name for Puerto Rico itself, Borinquen (Land of the Noble Lord), also survives and many Puerto Rican people take pride in referring to themselves as *boricua* (a word derived from Borinquen). In fact, the Puerto Rican official anthem is entitled "La Borinqueña" (Land of Borinquen).

Columbus named the island San

Juan Bautista and Spain claimed it as part of its colonial territory. The capital of Puerto Rico, San Juan, was originally called Puerto Rico (Rich Port) because Spain realized that the city was a good base for naval operations. In time, there was a switch and the entire country was known as Puerto Rico, while the city became known as San Juan.

In the 16th century, Spain started to settle the land, forcing the Tainos to mine for gold. Before the middle of the century, the gold was gone and the Taino were dying out from diseases brought by the Europeans. The Spanish brought slaves from Africa to cultivate sugar cane. Spanish men had children with Taino and African women. The children with Spanish and indigenous heritage were referred to as *mestizo*. The society was divided

During the Spanish colonial period, the Puerto Rican economy was based on agriculture. This included plantations where labor-intensive crops like sugar cane and tobacco were grown, as well as ranches for raising livestock.

American warships under the command of Admiral William Sampson bombard San Juan in May 1898. U.S. troops would later invade and capture the island. In the treaty that ended the Spanish-American War, Spain turned control of Puerto Rico over to the United States.

into three groups: Spaniards, **Creoles** (at the time, this was the term for Spanish people born in a Spanish colony and not in the motherland) were the ruling class; the mestizos were in the middle; and slaves or any free people of African descent were at the lowest level.

By the early 19th century, Spain was no longer as powerful as it had been in previous centuries. Puerto Ricans noticed this and took the opportunity to press the Spanish government for more independence. First, the island was allowed to hold elections and then islanders became citizens of Spain and could send someone to Spain to represent them. But the effects of these gains were lost since Spain decided to appoint unjust governors to govern Puerto Rico. Spain lost control over Puerto Rico and some of its other colonies to the U.S. in 1898, after the Spanish-American war ended.

The pattern for rule in Puerto Rico that began with Spain continued with the U.S. Over time, islanders were granted more rights but not complete control. Like Spain, the U.S. saw the value in using Puerto Rico for its navy and as a place for producing crops like sugar but did not invest in *infrastructure*.

The people of Puerto Rico have long fought for independence. The Spanish quickly ended a Taino rebellion in 1511. In 1868, Puerto Ricans who wanted independence took over the town of Lares, and again Spain put an end to the rebellion. During the Nationalist Insurrection of 1950, there were attempts to assassinate Luis Muñoz Marín, Puerto Rico's governor and U.S. President Harry Truman. And in 1954, Puerto Rican Nationalists opened fire in the visitor gallery of the U.S. House of Representatives in Washington D.C., wounding five Congressmen.

Under the rule of the U.S., some Puerto Ricans want full statehood;

Tourists disembark from a cruise ship docked in San Juan. Tourism is an important part of Puerto Rico's economy, but the island has also become an important center of industry.

In 2012, Puerto Ricans voted in a referendum on their status. Fifty-four percent of the voters said they no longer wanted to be a U.S. territory, while 46 percent were happy with the current status. In a follow-up question, 61 percent of the respondents wanted Puerto Rico to be admitted as a state, while just 5 percent wanted complete independence.

some want increased rights as a commonwealth; and still others want complete independence from the United States.

For years, The U.S. Navy used Vieques, an island off the coast of Puerto Rico's mainland for bombing practice. Before the U.S. starting using the island for military purposes, Vieques had a thriving fishing industry but that industry suffered once the U.S. Navy arrived. After the U.S. Navy began bombing practice and stored old weapons on the island, many inhabitants of Vieques could not make a living or they found the conditions unbearable. So, they migrated to other parts of Puerto Rico and other parts of the world. After years of protests, a civilian guard was killed in a military exercise in 1999 and opposition to the U.S. presence on Vieques intensified. The U.S. decided to stop military operations in 2003 and closed its naval base on Vieques in 2004. The island is now a nature preserve and tourist destination.

Government

In 1952, Puerto Rico became a Commonwealth or freely associated state of the United States. In this arrangement, Puerto Rico has its own constitution that it can change if needed but Puerto Rican laws cannot oppose the U.S. Constitution. Puerto Ricans can be drafted to serve in the U.S. military if the United States goes to war.

All Puerto Ricans are U.S. citizens and have U.S. passports, but they cannot cast votes in U.S. presidential elections while living on the island. Puerto Ricans that move to the U.S, mainland can vote for President and members of Congress and they are also required to pay federal taxes.

The Resident Commissioner, a representative Puerto Rico sends to the U.S. House of Representatives, can speak before the House and work on committees but cannot vote for bills to become law. Puerto Rico does not send a representative to the U.S. Senate.

The Capitol of Puerto Rico is located near Old San Juan. The building is home to the commonwealth's legislative assembly.

Some Famous Puerto Ricans

Pedro Albizu Campos (1891–1965), president of the Nationalist Party, fought fiercely for Puerto Rican independence. He was elected in 1920. Albizu Campos planned the Nationalist Insurrection of 1950 and spent the final years of his life in prison. He was beloved even by people who didn't share is views because he believed so strongly in Puerto Rico.

Rita Moreno

More than 230 Puerto Rican baseball players have appeared in the major leagues since the 1940s. Roberto Clemente (1934–1972) won four National League batting titles and accumulated 3,000 hits during his career. He was killed while on a mission of mercy to Nicaragua. Clemente was elected to the National Baseball Hall of Fame in 1973. Other Hall-of-Famers include Orlando Cepeda (b. 1937) and Roberto Alomar (b. 1968), both of whom were born in Ponce. Yadier Molina (b. 1982) of the St. Louis Cardinals is considered one of the best catchers in the major leagues today. Carlos Beltran (b. 1977) was elected to eight all-star teams during his career.

Multi-talented Rita Moreno (b. 1931) has won Emmy, Tony, Oscar, and Grammy awards. One of her best-known roles was Anita in the movie musical *West Side Story*.

Tito Puente (1923–2000), known as the "King of Latin Jazz," was a masterful musician and bandleader who blended Latin music with other musical styles and won five Grammy Awards.

Yadier Molina

In 2009, Sonia Sotomayor (b. 1954) became the first Latina to become a justice on the U.S. Supreme Court. Sotomayor, the daughter of Puerto Ricans who moved to New York City, was the third woman to serve on the nation's highest court.

Pop singer Enrique "Ricky" Martin (b. 1971) is one of the best-selling artists of all time, with more than 85 million albums sold. His hits include "Livin' la Vida Loca" and "The Cup of Life."

Puerto Ricans elect a Governor as head of their executive branch. The governor has a four-year term and there are no term limits. Next in the chain of command is the secretary of state who acts as governor if the governor leaves the island and would become governor if the governor dies or resigns.

Like the United States, Puerto Rico has a bicameral legislature with a house of representatives and a senate. All members of Puerto Rico's legislative branch serve for four years.

The Economy

Both Spain and the U.S. were more interested in how Puerto Rico could benefit them than in how they could help the island prosper. Under Spanish rule through the 16th, 17th,

and part of the 18th centuries, Puerto Ricans were only allowed to trade with Spain and this put the island at a disadvantage. After the U.S. took control of Puerto Rico, U.S. companies purchased a lot of land and farmers who had been independent then had little choice but to cultivate sugarcane and other crops for low wages. Puerto Rico was a leading producer of sugar, coffee, and tobacco but the majority of Puerto Ricans remained poor.

Luis Muñoz Marín, the first Puerto Rican governor elected by the people, initiated an effort called Operation Bootstrap after World War II to help the island shifts its focus from agriculture to manufacturing. One major *component* of Operation Bootstrap was encouraging U.S. companies to set up operations in Puerto Rico in exchange for *tax breaks*.

Since the Puerto Rican economy is linked the the U.S. economy, the island was affected by the recession that hit the U.S. in the mid-2000s. Puerto Rico still generates revenue from exporting rum and from tourism but its economy has suffered in recent years.

 Did You Know?

One of the uninhabited islands off the coast of Puerto Rico is named Caja de Muertos (Dead Man's Chest).

New York governor Andrew Cuomo was one of 80,000 marchers who participated in the 57th annual Puerto Rico Day Parade in New York City in 2014. New York has a vibrant Puerto Rican community.

Colorfully painted houses line an alley in Old San Juan.

The People

As a Spanish colony, Puerto Rican society was divided among racial and class lines and some of those divisions still exist. As far as ethnicity, most Puerto Ricans are Hispanic or Latino but all do not have the same racial background. According the Census Bureau's 2013 American Community Survey, most Puerto Ricans identify as white. The next largest group is those who identify as black and the third largest group is those who identify as American Indian. Fewer people in the survey identified themselves as belonging to two or more racial groups but that doesn't mean that Puerto Ricans don't recognize their mixture of cultural identities.

Puerto Rico's connection to the United States also plays an important role in how the Puerto Rican people see themselves. American culture has had a lot of influence on Puerto Rico. No matter which side they take in the debate about Puerto Rican independence, most Puerto Ricans have either spent time in the United States or know someone who has. Although Puerto Ricans can be found in all 50

Scenic view of San Juan, the largest city in Puerto Rico.

Ponce, Puerto Rico's second-largest city, has a population of about 170,000.

states, a large concentration of them chose to settle in the New York City area during a big wave of migration in the middle of the 20th century.

In New York City, people who left Puerto Rico created a new identity that blends the culture of the island with that of their new home and they sometimes refer to themselves as **Nuyorican**. Some Puerto Ricans move to the United States to stay. Others return to Puerto Rico, sometimes to retire, and they bring with them habits and customs from the United States.

Major Cities

Most Puerto Ricans live in cities that were founded near the coast.

San Juan, the capital of Puerto Rico, is divided between Old San Juan and the modern city that grew out of the 16th century port town. Old San Juan still has cobblestones and buildings that reflect the architecture of the colonial era. In Old San Juan, you can see El Morro and La Fortaleza, military fortresses built by the Spanish that offer great views of San Juan Bay. There is also La Casa Blanca (The White House). This building, constructed in 1521, first served as a fortress and later became the home of Ponce de Leon, the island's first governor. San Juan also has art galleries, museums, and places to shop.

Near San Juan is the city of *Bayamón*. This progressive city is home to Luis A. Ferré Science Park, a 42-acre park with museums, play-grounds, and a zoo all dedicated to the theme of scientific exploration. Bayamón is also known as El Pueblo de Chicharrón (Fried Pork Rind City).

The city of *Ponce*, which was founded in the late 17th century by Ponce de Leon's great-grandson, has worked to preserve its colonial heritage and draw tourists. There are a number of historical museums and one of the most photographed buildings is the Parque de Bombas. This red and black wooden firehouse was built for an exposition in 1882 and was used by the city's fire department until it was closed in 1989. The following year it opened as a museum.

Further Reading

Burgan, Michael. *Puerto Rico and Other Outlying Areas*. Milwaukee: World Almanac, 2003.

Jiménez de Wagenheim, Olga. *Puerto Rico: An Interpretive History from Pre-Columbian Times to 1900*. Princeton, NJ: Markus Wiener Publishers, 1998.

Pierce Flores, Lisa. *The History of Puerto Rico*. Santa Barbara, CA: Greenwood Press, 2010.

Internet Resources

http://www.topuertorico.org

> Welcome to Puerto Rico! offers information on the history, government, geography, and culture of Puerto Rico.

https://www.cia.gov/library/publications/the-world-factbook/geos/rq.html

> The CIA World Factbook is a regularly updated resource that provides a wealth of demographic information about Puerto Rico.

http://www.seepuertorico.com/

> This website provides information about Puerto Rico for those interested in visiting the island.

 # Text-Dependent Questions

1. Which indigenous group inhabited Puerto Rico when Columbus arrived?
2. What was the purpose of Operation Bootstrap?
3. What are some of the differences between being a Commonwealth and being a state?

Research Project

Puerto Rican governor Luis Muñoz Marín pardoned Nationalist leader Pedro Albizu Campos. Use the Internet and the library to research these two leaders. Write a one-page report about their different approaches to leadership in Puerto Rico.

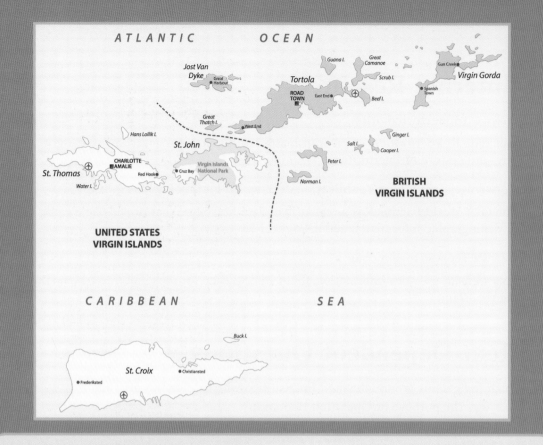

U.S. Virgin Islands at a Glance

Area: 738 sq miles (1,910 sq km)[1]
   Land: 134 sq miles (346 sq km)
  Water: 604 sq miles (1,564 sq km)
Highest elevation: Crown Mountain,
  1,556 feet (474 m)
Lowest elevation: sea level

Capital: Charlotte Amalie
Population: 106,405[2]

Official bird: yellow breast
Official flower: yellow elder

[1] *U.S. Census Bureau.* [2] *U.S. Census Bureau*

U.S. Virgin Islands

When Christopher Columbus saw the numerous islands that lie east of Puerto Rico between the Caribbean Sea and the Atlantic Ocean, he was reminded of the Catholic saint Ursula. According to legend, Ursula was a princess. She and thousands of attending maidens were attacked and died on a sea voyage as she was (depending on the story) either on her way to get married, or avoiding a marriage to a man she did not feel was suitable. Columbus named the island group Las Once Mil Virgenes ("Eleven Thousand Virgins") in honor of St. Ursula. Today, we know this land as the Virgin Islands.

Geography

The three main islands in the Virgin Islands—St. Thomas, St. John, and St. Croix—are mountainous, with St. Croix being the flattest. The mountainous *terrain* combined with a lack of rivers and streams makes it difficult to farm on the island. This does not mean that the island lacks plant life, however. There are numerous plant species. Animals also thrive on the Virgin Islands, with

Did You Know?

The U.S. Virgin Islands should not be confused with the British Virgin Islands, which are to the east. There are thirty-six islands in the British Virgin Islands and these islands are a British colony.

Virgin Islands National Park covers much of the island of St. John and extends offshore. Visitors can take in the *lush* scenery on land and see underwater gardens. The park also preserves stone objects from the island's long-ago indigenous inhabitants as well as ruins from the colonial era.

History

more that 220 species of birds as well as lizards, iguanas, and land crabs. The waters around the islands contain fascinating underwater sights like coral reef, fish in vibrant colors, and hundreds of types of shells.

The Ciboney Indians are the first group scholars are aware of to settle in the Virgin Islands. They were *nomads* from South America. Next came the Arawak Indians. It is believed that the Arawak traveled to the Virgin Islands

Words to Understand in This Chapter

civilians—people who are not a part of the military.
lush—healthy, full of life.
nomads—people who move to different places and do not have a permanent home.
supplant—to take the place of someone or something.
terrain—an area of land with distinct geographic features.

View of Cruz Bay, the largest town on the island of St. John, and an important commercial center for the U.S. Virgin Islands. The town has a population of about 2,800.

A diver explores a coral reef off the coast of St. Croix.

The harbor at St. Thomas, one of the islands that make up the U.S. Virgin Islands. Almost half of this territory's population lives on St. Thomas.

from Venezuela using canoes that had sails.

The Arawak are thought to be peaceful in contrast to the next group to arrive: the Caribs. The Caribs arrived during the 15th century and treated the Arawak cruelly.

After Columbus visited the islands in 1493, Spain did not establish a permanent settlement there. Still, the arrival of Europeans and exposure to the diseases they carried with them meant the end of the Caribs and any Arawak that remained. It wasn't until the 1600s that Denmark and England created the first European settlements there. Denmark and England would wrestle over control of the islands in the 17th and 18th centuries. Pirates like Blackbeard and Captain Kidd operated out of St. Thomas as they attacked ships passing through the area.

The Danes and the English brought in African slaves to work on plantations that grew sugar, cotton, and tobacco. St. Thomas was home to a large slave market. In 1733, slaves on St. Thomas decided to rebel and

Did You Know?

In Christiansted and Frederiksted on the island of St. Croix, buildings are numbered consecutively (1,2,3, etc.) on one side of the street throughout each city. Numbers then begin again consecutively on the opposite side of the street.

took over the island for about half a year until French soldiers defeated them.

During the 19th century, the United States became interested in buying the islands from Denmark. An offer was made in 1867, but the two countries couldn't agree on a price. The U.S. tried again in 1902, but again was rebuffed. In 1917, during World War I, the U.S. government wanted to purchase the islands in order to establish naval bases. They wanted to prevent enemies from attacking American ships traveling through the Panama Canal. Denmark sold the islands to the U.S. for $25 million in gold.

Some Famous Virgin Islanders

One of the Founding Fathers of the United States, Alexander Hamilton (1757–1804), spent his teen years on St. Croix, where he worked as a clerk. Hamilton was a hero of the American Revolution, played an instrumental role in the ratification of the U.S. Constitution in 1787, and as the first Secretary of the U.S. Treasury he helped to establish the American financial system.

Basketball player Tim Duncan (b. 1976) hails from the island of St. Croix. He led the San Antonio Spurs to five NBA titles, and won the league's Most Valuable Player award twice.

Alexander Hamilton

Best known for playing the character of Dr. Frasier Crane on two sitcoms (*Cheers* and *Frasier*), Kelsey Grammer (b. 1955) was born on the island of St. Thomas. He is an actor, writer, producer, and director.

Government

After the U.S. purchased the Virgin Islands in 1916, the Navy was in charge of the islands until 1954, when the U.S. Department of the Interior took over.

As inhabitants of an unincorporated territory of the United States, the people of the Virgin Islands were granted U.S. citizenship in 1927. However, they cannot vote for the U.S. president. Since 1970, the people of the Virgin Islands have elected a governor for a four-year term.

The U.S. Virgin Islands's Senate was created as a result of the Organic Act of 1936. There are 15 senators in the legislature, and these senators serve for two-year terms.

The U.S. president appoints a federal district judge to serve the Virgin Islands. Islanders also send a nonvoting delegate to the U.S. House of Representatives.

The Economy

The Virgin Islands once relied heavily on sugar cane and other crops as the mainstay of its economy but now farming and crop production have been *supplanted* by tourism.

Airfields built for military use during World War II laid the ground for a tourism industry. Once *civilians* were allowed to use these airfields, it became possible to attract tourists to the islands. The Virgin Islands also have ports that allow cruise ships to dock and bring in tourists. In the 1950s, the islands saw about 15,000 tourists each year. Now more than a

Charlotte Amalie, located on the island of St. Thomas, is the capital and largest city of the U.S. Virgin Islands. Once a haven for pirates, today it is one of the busiest tourist ports in the Caribbean.

The stone tower pictured here is known as Blackbeard's Castle. It was actually built in the 1670s by Danish soldiers, so they could watch for approaching ships. The castle has long been associated with the 18th century pirate Edward "Blackbeard" Teach, who according to legend used it as a base of operations. Today it is a national historic landmark, and is on the grounds of a small hotel and resort on the island of St. Thomas.

The entrance to the office of the legislature of the U.S. Virgin Islands. The legislature is made up of 15 senators, who are each elected to two-year terms.

A large cricket complex on the island of St. Croix. Cricket is a popular sport in the U.S. Virgin Islands, as it is in many other Caribbean islands.

million tourists visit the islands in a year. In addition to providing jobs in the hospitality industry, tourism allows related industries such as construction to offer employment.

The People

Most of the indigenous people of these islands were wiped out during the colonial era. The descendants of the Africans that European settlers brought to work the land form the majority of the islands' population today. According to the U.S. Census Bureau, about 76 percent of Virgin Islanders are black or African American. The total population of the islands is about 107,000.

While census data might indicate that many of the inhabitants of the

Virgin Islands are of African descent, that is not the whole story. Many are black but not all are native to the island. The Virgin Islands experienced a population boom between 1960 and 1990—there were more births and an increase in immigration. Residents of other Caribbean islands chose to make the U.S. Virgin Islands their home because of the greater opportunities to be found there.

Major Cities

Charlotte Amalie, a city named for a Danish queen, is the capital of St. Thomas. Although the Danes are gone, visitors to Charlotte Amalie can still see the Danish influence in the architecture. Tourists can enjoy natural scenery, shopping, dining, and entertainment. Visitors appreciate the beauty of the beaches near the city and fishermen appreciate the quality of fish found in the waters nearby.

Visitors to **Christiansted**, the largest town on the island of St. Croix, can take a walking tour to see a fort and 18th century warehouses that are on the U.S, National Register of Historic Places.

Further Reading

Dookhan, Isaac. *A History of the Virgin Islands of the United States*. Kingston, Jamaica: Canoe Press, 2002.

Porter, Darwin and Danforth Prince. *Frommer's Virgin Islands*, 11th Edition. Hoboken, NJ: John Wiley & Sons, Inc., 2011.

Singer, Gerald. *St. Thomas United States Virgin Islands*. St. John, United States Virgin Islands: Sombrero Publishing Company, 2007.

Internet Resources

http://virginislandsdailynews.com

The home page of the *Virgin Islands Daily News.*

http://www.visitusvi.com

This Web site is for travelers who wish to visit the Virgin Islands.

http://www.nps.gov/viis/index.htm

The is the National Park Service Web site for the Virgin Islands National Park.

 # Text-Dependent Questions

1. How did the Virgin Islands get their name?
2. Why did the U.S. decide to buy the Virgin Islands from Denmark?
3. Find a currency converter Web site or look up information in order to estimate what the price the U.S. paid for the Virgin Islands would be in dollars today.

 # Research Project

Pirates like Blackbeard and Captain Kidd were feared by those traveling by ship and there are a lot of legends about their adventures. Using the Internet or your school library, research what is fact and what is fiction about these pirates. Make a chart comparing what is considered true and what may be fiction.

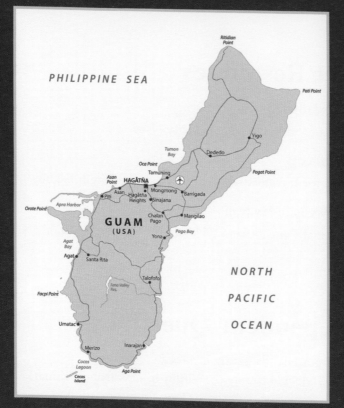

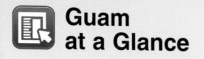

Guam at a Glance

Area: 210 sq miles (544 sq km)[1]
   Land: 210 sq miles (544 sq km)
   Water: 0 sq miles (0 sq km)
Highest elevation: Mount Lamlam,
   1,332 feet (402 m)
Lowest elevation: sea level

Capital: Hagatna
Population: 159,358[2]

Official bird: Mariana fruit dove
Official flower: Bougainvillea

[1] U.S. Census Bureau. [2] U.S. Census Bureau

Guam

The island of Guam narrows in the middle and its shape reminds some people of a human footprint or a peanut. Guam is the largest and southernmost island in the Mariana Islands *archipelago*. Located in the North Pacific Ocean, Guam sits between Hawaii and the Philippines. This location made it an important stopping point for ships that were crossing the Pacific.

The Marianas Trench, the deepest point in the ocean, is not far from the coast of Guam. The trench is nearly 6.8 miles (11 km) deep.

Geography

Guam was formed by volcanic eruptions and in its earliest stages, much of the island was covered by water. Once the volcano became less active, coral reefs formed and you can find coral reefs on its coast today. The coastline is steep on the northern part of the island but the northern interior is a flat plateau. Most of the island's rivers are found in the mountainous south.

Guam is no longer volcanically active. However, because the island is located near the point where two tectonic plates meet, the region around Guam is subject to occasional earthquakes. In September 2014, a major earthquake struck just 25 miles (40 km) away from Guam. However, it caused little damage, and was too deep in the ocean to trigger a tsunami, or tidal wave.

Tropical plants that populate the coast include coconut palms and screw pine. There are forests on the island's northern plateau and sword grass in the south.

Guam has a warm and humid climate with a dry season and a wet season. The island is vulnerable dangerous *typhoons*, which tend to hit between May and October each year.

History

Before Europeans arrived, Guam was inhabited by the Chamorro people. There is much that is unknown about the Chamorros but they did leave behind stone pillars known as latte stones. These stone pillars that the Chamorro rested their houses upon can be found all over the island. Explorers who visited Guam were impressed by the Chamorros' craftmanship, describing them as skilled at

 Words to Understand in This Chapter

archipelago—an island group.

influx—a large number of people or a large amount of things.

masonry—craftsmanship completed using stone, brick, or cement.

matrilineal—descending from the mother's side of a family.

prestige—respect, admiration; having a good reputation in the eyes of others.

strategic—helpful in carrying out a plan or reaching a goal.

typhoon—name given to powerful tropical storms in the Pacific or Indian Oceans.

unicameral—describes a government assembly that has a single legislative body.

Mount Lamlam is the highest mountain peak in Guam, rising 1,332 feet (402 m) above sea level. Lamlam *is a Chamorro word meaning "lightning."*

woodworking, stonework, and *masonry*. Before the arrival of Europeans, Chamorros divided themselves into *matrilineal* clans. Class and rank were important to the ancient Chamorros. For example, when they traveled using canoes, only people of high rank were allowed to steer. Scholars also believe that the Chamorros used shells and iron for bartering.

The explorer Ferdinand Magellan arrived in Guam in 1521, traveling from South America. Magellan nicknamed the land Island of Thieves, because he claimed the natives stole many items from his ship.

Magellan had been exploring the Pacific for Spain, which claimed Guam in the 1560s. However, the Spanish did not make it into a thriving

Two U.S. officers plant an American flag on Guam eight minutes after U.S. Marines and Army assault troops landed on the Pacific island on July 20, 1944

colony. Instead, Guam was largely neglected and used as a place for Spanish ships to stop when they were traveling between the prosperous colonies of New Spain (Mexico) and the Philippines.

Guam would become one of the first islands in the Pacific with a significant settlement of Europeans after missionaries from Spain came to the island to convert its people to Christianity.

Life under Spanish rule was difficult for the Chamorro people. Many died from lack of food, in wars, or from diseases that the Europeans brought to the island.

In 1898, at the end of the Spanish-American War, Spain turned over its controlling interests in Guam and Puerto Rico to the United States. This war had its roots in the Cuban struggle for independence. After the Spanish-American War, the U.S. gained *prestige* as a world power while Spain lost prestige. Under U.S. rule, Guam became a naval base.

One of the reasons the U.S. became interested in Guam was its *strategic* position in the Pacific

Ocean. Guam's position in relation to Japan, the Philippines, Australia, and the Asian continent made it an ideal place for a naval base. However, Guam was isolated and there was concern that Japan would consider a strong American military presence on Guam to be a threat. That concern was valid—the island of Guam was unprepared when the Japanese attacked on December 8, 1941. The attack occurred at the same time as the Japanese attack on Pearl Harbor, and launched the United States into World War II.

The Japanese captured and occupied Guam in 1941, and held the island for three years. The years under Japan's harsh rule were very difficult for the Guamanian people.

A variety of combat aircraft are parked on a runway at Anderson Air Force Base, Guam. The island is also home to a U.S. Navy base and a U.S. Coast Guard base.

Did You Know?

Guam is "Where America's Day Begins." Since it is west of the International Date Line, it experiences the start of a new day before any other part of the U.S.

American forces fought to regain control of Guam in 1944. The battle caused a lot of damage to the island, especially the capital city, which had to be rebuilt once the war was over.

Government

Much like people who live in other U.S. territories, Guamanians are citizens of the United States but they do not have the right to vote in U.S. national elections.

In 1950, President Truman signed the Organic Act of Guam. This gave the people of Guam American citizenship, along with many (but not all) of the rights of who were born in the United States. Guam's legislature and civilian court system were also created by the Organic Act.

The Organic Act was amended in 1968 to allow the people of Guam to elect a governor. Guamanians elected their first governor in 1970. Guam's governor serves for four years, and can choose executive department heads that must be approved by the country's *unicameral* legislature. Members of the unicameral legislature are elected every two years. Guam also sends a nonvoting delegate to the U.S. House of Representatives.

Guam has its own district court that functions the way a district court does in the U.S. and the U.S. court of appeals and the Supreme Court can review its decisions.

The Economy

Guam is the site of Andersen Air Force Base, an important military installation. There are also U.S. Coast Guard units stationed in Guam. These military installations support the island's economy.

While it is not lacking in natural beauty, Guam does lack natural resources to produce the amount of food needed to feed the people there. Guamanians grow some food in the lowlands and in clearings in the forest. They also cultivate livestock and the island has expanded its fishing industry. Still, it is necessary for Guam to import food to feed the people who live there.

Tourism has been one way for Guam to improve its economy. With its pleasant climate, lush greenery, duty-free shopping, and historic sites, Guam attracts vacationers, especially from Japan. In recent years, Guam has attempted to do more to emphasize the Chamorro culture as a way of attracting tourists.

Construction has been one of Guam's leading industries. The island is also home to manufacturing companies that produce items like watches, furniture, tobacco products, and textiles.

The People

It is believed that Guam's indigenous people, the Chamorro, reached the island after migrating from Southeast Asia. The Guamanians of today are the descendants of the Chamorro and many also have European, East Asian, and Latin American ancestors as well. The descendants of the Chamorros make up less than half of the island's population.

Some Famous Guamanians

TV news journalist Ann Curry (b. 1956) was born in Guam to a Japanese mother and American father. She has been an anchor on *Dateline NBC* and a host of the *Today* show.

Chess grandmaster Ray Robson (b. 1994) was born in Guam. In 1989 as a teenager, he became the youngest Grandmaster to represent the U.S in international competition.

Hagatna is Guam's largest city.

In addition to Guamanians, some of the island's population comes from Hawaii and the Philippines. An *influx* of visitors and new residents began to arrive in Guam after 1962. This was the year when a security clearance was no longer required to enter Guam. The island also has a large population of people from the U.S. that work on its military installations.

Although English is the official language in Guam, older Guamanians still speak the language of their Chamorro ancestors.

The influence of Guam's years under Spanish rule are still evident in the architecture and the fact that many Guamanians still practice the Roman Catholic faith the Spanish brought to the island. The cultures of neighboring countries such as the Philippines also play a role in Guamanian life. And last but not least, the people of Guam also look to the U.S. and follow some of our customs.

Major City

The population of Guam is concentrated near the territory's capital, *Hagatna*. Hagatna was once called Agana. In 1998, the capital city's name was changed back to Hagatna, its original Chamorro name.

Efforts to improve the city during the last century were thwarted after a typhoon struck Hagatna in 1940. Japan's invasion, and fighting during World War II, also damaged the city. Many improvements were made to the city of Hagatna after World War II ended.

Today the city's historic sites are tourist attractions.

Further Reading

Carano, Paul and Pedro C. Sanchez. *A Complete History of Guam*. Rutland, VI: Charles E. Tuttle Company, 1964.

Cunningham, Lawrence J. and Janice J. Beaty. *Guam: A Natural History*. Honolulu, HI: Bess Press, Inc., 2001.

Rogers, Robert F. *Destiny's Landfall: A History of Guam*. Honolulu, HI: University of Hawai'i Press, 2011.

Internet Resources

http://www.guampedia.com

The homepage for Guampedia, a Web site focused on the history of Guam and of the Chamorro people.

http://www.guam.gov

Official Web site for the government of Guam.

http://www.visitguam.com

Official Web site of Guam Visitors Bureau.

Text-Dependent Questions

1. What evidence of the Chamorro people can still be seen in Guam today?
2. Why was the U.S. interested in controlling Guam?
3. How is Guam's legislature different from the U.S. legislature?

Research Project

The Treaty of Paris of 1898 is the agreement that gave the U.S. control over Guam. Learn more about this treaty. What other lands were included in this agreement?

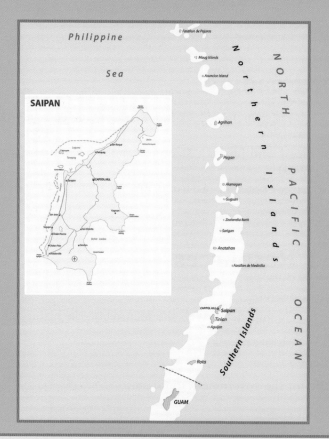

SAIPAN

Northern Marianas at a Glance

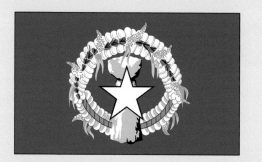

Area: 179 sq miles (464 sq km)[1]
   Land: 179 sq miles (464 sq km)
   Water: 0 sq miles (0 sq km)
Highest elevation: Agrihan volcano, 3,166 feet (965 m)
Lowest elevation: sea level

Capital: Saipan
Population: 53,883[2]

Official bird: Mariana Fruit-dove
Official flower: wood violet

[1] U.S. Census Bureau. [2] U.S. Census Bureau

Northern Mariana Islands

European explorers were impressed by the sailing ability of the Chamorro people as they first approached the Mariana Islands. However, there would be a misunderstanding between the Chamorros and explorer Ferdinand Magellan, who later referred to the islands as Islas de Ladrones (Islands of Thieves). The island group would eventually be renamed the Mariana Islands for Queen Mariana of Spain.

Most of the islands in the Northern Mariana Islands group are uninhabited. The three islands in the Northern Marianas territory that are inhabited are Saipan, Tinian, and Rota. According to the U.S. Census Bureau, 90 percent of the population of the Northern Mariana Islands lives on Saipan.

Guam is actually the largest of the entire Mariana Islands group but it is considered a separate territory from the Northern Mariana Islands.

Geography

Saipan, Tinian, and Rota are *limestone islands*, and are surrounded by coral reefs. Most of the uninhabited islands are located to

Did You Know?

The official name for this territory is the Commonwealth of the Northern Mariana Islands. These islands and Puerto Rico are the only U.S. territories to receive commonwealth status.

the north of Saipan, Tinian, and Rota. The uninhabited islands were formed by volcanic activity, and there are active volcanoes on Anatahan, Pagan, and Agrihan. The volcano on Agrihan is the highest point in the Northern Marianas territory, at 3,166 feet (965 m) above sea level.

Because the Northern Mariana Islands are located west of the International Date Line, the islands are one day ahead of the United States.

History

Ferdinand Magellan visited the Northern Mariana Islands in 1521 during his voyage around the world. Spain claimed the islands, and took control of them in 1546. The Spanish established farms on the islands, and used the largest island, Saipan, as a place for ships to stop for food and water during Pacific voyages.

Spain remained in control of the Northern Marianas until after the Spanish-American War in 1898, when Spain could no longer afford to manage them and sold the islands to

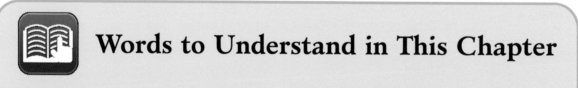

Words to Understand in This Chapter

limestone island—an island that is made primarily of the fossilized remains of ancient coral reefs, as opposed to an island created by volcanic activity.

referendum—a vote that the people of a county, state, or other voting body take to make a decision about an important issue.

Banzai Cliff is located near the village of San Roque on the island of Saipan. In July 1944, hundreds of Japanese soldiers and civilians leapt off the cliff to their deaths so they would not be captured by the American troops fighting for control of the island.

Germany. The islands became part of a German colony, but the Germans did little to settle or develop them.

In 1914, as World War I began, Japan captured the islands from Germany. At the end of the war, the League of Nations formally awareded control over the island group to Japan, which had fought on the side of the Allies during the conflict.

The American B-29 bomber Enola Gay lands at the air field on Tinian after dropping the first atomic bomb on Hiroshima, Japan, on August 6, 1945.

During World War II, the U.S. invaded the islands. Many soldiers were killed during the fight to gain control over Saipan in the summer of 1944, but U.S. forces soon gained control over both Saipan and Tinian. The military established air bases, which U.S. bombers used to attack the Japanese mainland.

With the approval of the United Nations, the U.S. took over administration of the islands when World War II ended. In 1975, the citizens of the Northern Mariana Islands voted on a *referendum* to become a self-govern-

ing commonwealth of the United States. Although this agreement was approved in 1976, it wasn't until 1986 that the islands received official status as a U.S. Commonwealth.

Government

The Northern Mariana Islands are a territory of the United States, and federal programs and funding is administered by the Office of Insular Affairs, an agency of the U.S. Department of the Interior. Residents of the Northern Mariana Islands are U.S. citizens, but are not represented in

Congress or permitted to vote in presidential elections.

Every four years, a governor is elected to oversee the Northern Marianas territory. Residents of the islands also elect representatives to the Northern Mariana Islands Commonwealth Legislature. This assembly has two houses: the Senate, with nine members elected to four-year terms, and the House of Representatives, with 20 members elected to two-year terms.

Most offices of the Northern Marianas government are located on Saipan. Because there are no large cities, and the 15 individual islands are organized as municipalities, Saipan is usually listed as the territorial capital.

The Economy

While the islands do export some crops like coconuts, breadfruit, and melons and also has seen growth in its textile industry, the Northern Mariana islands get their greatest economic gains from tourism.

The People

Like the people of Guam, many inhabitants of the Northern Mariana islands

A park on Rota, the smallest of the inhabited islands of the Northern Marianas territory. Rota covers about 33 square miles (85 sq km) and has a population of about 4,000.

A tourist resort on the coast of Saipan.

are descended from the Chamorro people. However, the U.S. Census Bureau found that Filipinos are the largest overall ethnic group in the Northern Mariana Islands, making up over 29 percent of the population. The Chinese-American population, at over 22 percent, is also greater than that of the indigenous Chamorros, at 21 percent. The island is also home to people who are descendants of the Carolinians, another indigenous group.

The majority of the people of these islands are Roman Catholic, due to their history as a Spanish colony.

Communities

Saipan is home to about 30 villages. The territorial government is based in **Capitol Hill**, which has a population of 1,000. **Garapan** offers shopping, dining, and entertainment for tourists. The only lake on Saipan is located near the village of **Susupe**.

Further Reading

Goodridge, Walt. *Saipan Living*. New York: Passion Profit, 2013.

Prefer, Nathan. *The Battle for Tinian: Vital Stepping Stone in America's War Against Japan*. Havertown, Pa.: Casemate Publishers, 2012.

Rock, Tim. *Diving and Snorkeling Guide to Guam and the Northern Mariana Islands*. Guam: Manta Ray Publishing, 2012.

Internet Resources

http://www.mymarianas.com

> The Mariana Visitors Authority offers information on recreation for visitors to the islands.

http://gov.mp

> This is the official Web site for the government of the Northern Mariana Islands.

 # Text-Dependent Questions

1. Why did the U.S. invade the Northern Mariana Islands during World War II?
2. What event allowed the Northern Mariana Islands to become a commonwealth of the U.S.?
3. What is the time difference between the U.S. and the Northern Mariana Islands?

 # Research Project

Get more information about Queen Mariana, the woman for whom the Northern Mariana Islands were named. Which famous painter created portraits of the queen and members of her family?

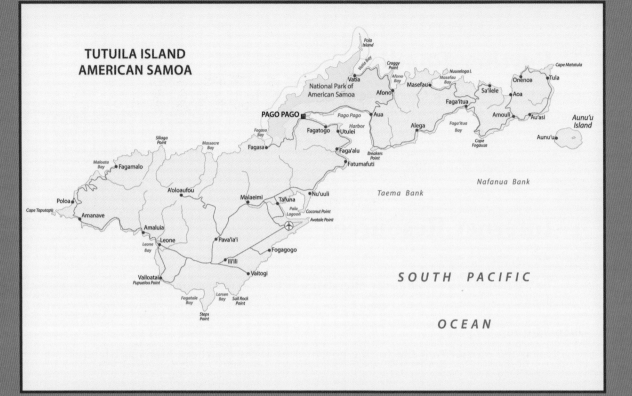

TUTUILA ISLAND
AMERICAN SAMOA

Pola Island

Craggy Point

National Park of American Samoa

Vaisa Bay

Vatia

Afono Bay

Afono

Masefau

Nauseloga I.

Masefau Bay

Sa'ilele

Onenoa • Tula

Cape Matatula

PAGO PAGO

Fagasa Bay

Fagatogo

Pago Pago

Harbor

Utulei

Aua

Alega

Faga'itua

Faga'itua Bay

Amouli

Au'asi

Aoa

Aunu'u

Island

Siliaga Point

Massacre Bay

Fagasa

Faga'alu

Fatumafuti

Breakers Point

Cape Fogausa

Aunu'u

Maloata Bay

Fagamalo

A'oloaufou

Malaeimi

Tafuna

Nu'uuli

Pala Lagoon

Coconut Point

Nafanua Bank

Taema Bank

Poloa

Cape Taputapu

Amanave

Amaluia

Leone

Leone Bay

Pava'ia'i

Avatale Point

Fogagogo

Ili'ili

Vaitogi

SOUTH PACIFIC

Vailoatai

Pupualoa Point

Fagatale Bay

Larsen Bay

Sail Rock Point

OCEAN

Steps Point

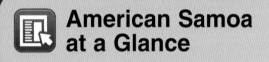

American Samoa at a Glance

Area: 77 sq miles (199 sq km)[1]
   Land: 77 sq miles (199 sq km)
   Water: 0 sq miles (0 sq km)
Highest elevation: Lata Mountain, 3,163 feet (964 m)
Lowest elevation: sea level

Capital: Pago Pago
Population: 55,519[2]

Official bird: Pacific imperial pigeon
Official flower: paogo

[1] U.S. Census Bureau. [2] U.S. Census Bureau

American Samoa

The original inhabitants of American Samoa and their descendants are Polynesian and share an ethnic background with native Hawaiians.

Geography

The group of islands in the South Pacific Ocean known as Samoa is divided into an independent state of Samoa and American Samoa. American Samoa is to the east and includes Tutuila (its largest island), Aunu'u, and Swains Island, which is a coral *atoll*.

American Samoa has a tropical climate, as it is located not far from the equator. On the coast, the temperature remains around 80° Fahrenheit (27° Celsius) throughout the year.

The Samoan archipelago gets a lot of rain—sometimes the island of Tutuila can get 200 inches (508 cm) of rain in a year. Samoans see the most rain from December to April. This is also the time of year when tropical *cyclones* are more likely.

The National Park of American Samoa is divided into three parts: one part on the island of Tutuila, one part on the island of

Tau, and an offshore coral reef and small part of shoreline on the island of Ofu. The park was established to preserve and protect coral reefs, tropical rainforests, and the animals that live there, as well as the traditional Samoan culture.

History

There is evidence that the earliest settlers of Samoa were, travelers from the Melanesian islands that arrived during the first millennium BCE. These early settlers of American Samoa may have had ancestors from Southeast Asia.

Dutch navigator Jacob Roggeveen is thought to be the first European to see Samoa but he did not stop long when he passed though in 1722.

It was French explorer Louis Antoine de Bougainville who decided to name the archipelago "Navigators' Islands" after reaching Samoa in 1768. However, there was no European settlement in the Samoan archipelago until 1830, when a British missionary named John Williams arrived in an attempt to convert the Samoan people to Christianity.

From 1838 to 1842, Lieutenant

 ## Words to Understand in This Chapter

annex—to add an area to a country or state, usually by taking control of that area.

arable—suitable for growing crops.

atoll—a ring-shaped island made of coral.

canning—the act of preserving food by sealing it in an airtight metal can.

coaling station—a safe place for a ship to stop and get more coal fuel. Before ships used oil as fuel, they needed coaling stations because it was not practical to carry the coal necessary for travel.

cyclone—a powerful storm with high winds.

matai—leader or chief of a family group in a Samoan system that goes back to early settlers of the island.

The rocky shoreline of Vatia Bay on Tutuila Island.

A U.S. Coast Guard ship approaches the entrance to Pago Pago Harbor.

Charles Wilkes commanded a small American naval fleet on an exploration of the South Pacific Ocean. Wilkes stopped at Samoa in 1839. During the 19th century, ships from the United States and Europe would stop regularly at Samoa when crossing the Pacific.

In 1872, Commander Richard W. Meade and a Samoan high chief named Mauga came to an agreement so American warships could use the island of Pago Pago as a **coaling station**. This agreement not only allowed the U.S. access to the island, it was also a way to discourage other countries from taking an interest in Samoa. At the time, coaling stations were important for a country with a navy because ships needed to refuel.

Other countries, especially Germany and Great Britain, were interested in Samoa as well because of

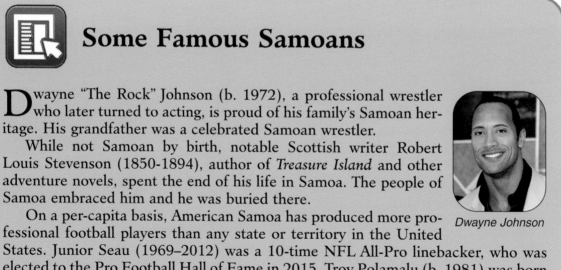

Some Famous Samoans

Dwayne "The Rock" Johnson (b. 1972), a professional wrestler who later turned to acting, is proud of his family's Samoan heritage. His grandfather was a celebrated Samoan wrestler.

While not Samoan by birth, notable Scottish writer Robert Louis Stevenson (1850-1894), author of *Treasure Island* and other adventure novels, spent the end of his life in Samoa. The people of Samoa embraced him and he was buried there.

On a per-capita basis, American Samoa has produced more pro-

Dwayne Johnson

fessional football players than any state or territory in the United States. Junior Seau (1969–2012) was a 10-time NFL All-Pro linebacker, who was elected to the Pro Football Hall of Fame in 2015. Troy Polamalu (b. 1981) was born in California to Samoan parents. The NFL Defensive Player of the Year in 2010, he is considered to be one of the greatest safeties of all time.

American servicemen watch Samoans perform a traditional dance.

its strategic location. During the late 1880s, Germany and the United States took sides in a civil war among Samoan tribes. Eventually, in 1899 the United States and Germany signed a treaty in which the Samoan archipelago was divided into two territories: German Samoa and American Samoa.

After this, the U.S. government negotiated with chiefs of the eastern islands in order to gain control of Tutuila, Aunu'u, and the Manua islands. These negotiations occurred between 1900 and 1904. However, the U.S. Congress did not officially accept the agreements until 1929.

Pola island rises over 400 feet (122 m) straight out of the ocean off Tutuila. The small island is an ideal nesting site for many species of seabirds.

Great Britain controlled Swains Island until 1925, when the U.S. *annexed* the small coral atoll.

Government

Samoa is under the jurisdiction of the U.S. Department of the Interior. It is an unincorporated territory. Samoans are U.S. citizens, but cannot vote in U. S. national elections.

Samoans elect a governor to oversee the territory. The governor has the power to veto laws made by the island's legislative body, the Fono. And the Fono must approve people that the governor appoints to oversee government departments.

The Fono is bicameral—it includes a Senate and House of Representatives. Senators are selected from the *matais* (family chiefs) and serve for four years. Representatives serve for two years, and are chosen by the people. Swains Island sends a delegate to the Samoan House of Representatives, but this delegate cannot vote.

The Economy

Samoa's lack of *arable* land and position as a U.S. territory have made it difficult for agriculture to flourish. Food must be imported to supplement the fruits and vegetables grown on the islands.

The tuna processing industry, which includes both fishing and **canning**, employs are large number of Samoans. Canned tuna is one of Samoa's main exports.

There has been an effort to bring more tourism to Samoa. The National Park of American Samoa was created in 1993 to further the tourism industry.

Rainmaker Mountain is a natural landmark located across from Pago Pago harbor.

The People

In ancient times, Samoans excelled at maritime arts such as boat building and navigation. They lived in family groups, with a matai in charge of an extended family.

The Samoan language was unwritten until the 19th century, when missionaries developed a written version based on the Latin alphabet. It is believed to be the oldest Polynesian language that has survived until today. Most Samoans speak both their native language and English.

While Samoans were willing to adopt Christianity, they didn't give up their indigenous beliefs. Unlike some other territories where the Roman Catholic church dominates, Samoans belong to a number of different Christian denominations.

Major City

Pago Pago is the capital of American Samoa as well as its main port. The natural form of Pago Pago's harbor make it an excellent place to dock ships and this was one of the reasons so many countries were interested in controlling Samoa.

Further Reading

American Samoa Humanities Council. *A History of American Samoa*. Honolulu, HI: Bess Press, 2009.

Shaffer, J. Robert. *American Samoa: 100 Years Under the United States Flag*. St. Waipahu, HI: Island Heritage, 2000.

Talbot, Dorinda. *Lonely Planet Samoa: Independent and American Samoa*. 3rd. Ed. Melbourne, Australia: Lonely Planet, 1998.

Internet Resources

http://www.americansamoa.travel

This is the website for the American Samoa Visitors Bureau.

http://americansamoa.gov

American Samoan government's official website.

http://www.nps.gov/npsa/index.htm

The Web site for the National Park of Samoa has colorful photos and interesting trivia about American Samoa's natural resources.

 # Text-Dependent Questions

1. Samoans share an ethnic background with the inhabitants of which state?
2. Why were so many countries interested in Samoa in the late 19th century?
3. What is a matai?

Research Project

Using the Internet or your school library, research coaling stations. Find out what supplies besides coal ships took on at coaling stations. Write a one-page paper about why these stations were needed.

Index

Agana, GU. *See* Hagatna, GU
Albizu Campos, Pedro, 17, 23
American Samoa
  area of, 54
  cities in, 61
  climate of, 55
  economy of, 60–61
  famous people from, 58
  geography of, 55–56
  government of, 60
  history of, 56, 58–60
  population of, 54, 61
  and tourism, 61
Arawak people, 8, 10, 26, 29
Archaics, 10
Aunu'u, AS, 55, 59

Bayamón, PR, 22
birds, official, 6, 24, 36, 46, 54
Borinquen. *See* Puerto Rico
Bougainville, Louis Antoine de, 56
British Virgin Islands, 26

Caja de Muertos, 18
  See also Puerto Rico
Carib Indians, 8, 11, 29
Chamorro people, 38–39, 40, 43, 47, 52
Charlotte Amalie, VI, 24, *31*, 34
Christiansted, St. Croix, 29, 34
Ciboney Indians, 26
climate, 7, 38, 55
Columbus, Christopher, 10–12, 25, 29
Commonwealth of Puerto Rico. *See* Puerto Rico
Commonwealth of the Northern Mariana Islands. *See* Northern Mariana Islands
coquí, 6, 8

Denmark, 29, *32*

economy
  of American Samoa, 60–61
  of Guam, 42
  of the Northern Mariana Islands, 51
  of Puerto Rico, 18
  of the Virgin Islands, 31, 33
England, 29, 58, 60

flowers, official, 6, 24, 36, 46, 54

Garapan, Northern Mariana Islands, 52
geography
  of American Samoa, 55–56
  of Guam, 37–38
  of the Northern Mariana Islands, 47–48
  of Puerto Rico, 7–9
  of the Virgin Islands, 25–26
Germany, 48–49, 58–59
government
  of American Samoa, 60
  of Guam, 42–43
  of the Northern Mariana Islands, 50–51
  of Puerto Rico, 15–16, 18
  of the Virgin Islands, 30, *32*
Guam
  area of, 36
  city in, 44
  climate of, 38
  economy of, 42
  famous people from, 43
  geography of, 37–38
  government of, 42–43
  history of, 38–42
  nicknames of, 39

population of, 36, 43–44
tourism in, 43

Hagatna, GU, 36, 44

Igneri (Saladoid) people, 10

Las Once Mil Virgenes. *See* Virgin Islands
Lata Mountain, AS, 54

Magellan, Ferdinand, 39, 47, 48
Manua, AS, 59
Mariana Islands. *See* Northern Mariana Islands
Marín, Luis Muñoz, 14, 18, 23
Mauga (Samoan high chief), 58
Meade, Richard W., 58
Mount Lamlam, GU, 36, *39*

National Park of American Samoa, 55–56
Nationalist Insurrection of 1950, 14, 17
"Navigators' Islands." *See* American Samoa
New York City, NY, *19*, 21
Northern Mariana Islands, 37
  area of, 46
  communities in the, 52–53
  economy of the, 51
  geography of the, 47–48
  government of, 50–51
  history of, 48–50
  islands in the, 47–48, 49, 50, 51
  nickname of, 47
  population of, 46, 51–52
  and tourism, 51

Ofu, AS, 56

Numbers in **bold italics** refer to captions.

Organic Act of Guam, 42
Ostionoid people, 10

Pago Pago, AS, 54, *57*, 58, 61
Ponce, PR, *21*, 22
population
    of American Samoa, 54, 61
    of Guam, 36, 43–44
    of the Northern Mariana
        Islands, 46, 51–52
    of Puerto Rico, 6, 20
    of the Virgin Islands, 24, *27*, *28*,
        33–34
Puerto Rico
    agriculture in, *12*, 18
    area of, 6
    cities in, 21–22
    climate of, 7
    economy of, 18
    famous people from, 17
    geography of, 7–9
    government of, 15–16, 18
    history of, 10–15, 40
    and independence, 14–15
    islands of, *9*, 15, 18

population of, 6, 20
tourism in, *14*, 15, 18, 22

research projects, 23, 35, 45, 53, 62
Roggeveen, Jacob, 56
Rota, Northern Mariana Islands, 46,
    47–48, *51*

Saipan, Northern Mariana Islands,
    46, 47–48, *49*, 50, 51, 52
San Juan, PR, 6, 10, 12, *13*, *16*, *19*,
    20, 21–22
San Juan Bautista. *See* Puerto Rico
slavery, 12–13, 29
Spain, 7–8, 11–14, 18, 29, 39–40,
    44, 48–49
Spanish-American War, 13, 40, 48
St. Croix, VI, 25, *27*, *33*, 34
St. John, VI, 25, 26, *27*
St. Thomas, VI, 25, *28*, *31*, *32*, 34
Swains Island, AS, 55, 60

Taino people, 10–11, 12, 14
Tau, AS, 56
Tinian, Northern Mariana Islands,

46, 47–48, 50
Truman, Harry, 14, 42
Tutuila, AS, 55, *57*, 59

U.S. Virgin Islands. *See* Virgin
    Islands

Vieques, *9*, 15
    See also Puerto Rico
Virgin Islands
    area of, 24
    cities in the, 29, 34
    economy of, 31, 33
    famous people from, 30
    geography of, 25–26
    government of, 30, *32*
    history of, 26, 29
    pirates in the, 29, *31*, *32*, 35
    population of, 24, *27*, *28*, 33–34
    tourism in the, 31, 33
Virgin Islands National Park, 26

Wilkes, Charles, 56, 58
Williams, John, 56

Series Glossary of Key Terms

bicameral—having two legislative chambers (for example, a senate and a house of representatives).

cede—to yield or give up land, usually through a treaty or other formal agreement.

census—an official population count.

constitution—a written document that embodies the rules of a government.

delegation—a group of persons chosen to represent others.

elevation—height above sea level.

legislature—a lawmaking body.

precipitation—rain and snow.

term limit—a legal restriction on how many consecutive terms an office holder may serve.